GENERAL SERIES 96

Franklin D. Roosevelt and the New Deal

D. K. ADAMS

The Historical Association

59a Kennington Park Road, London SE11 4JH

ACKNOWLEDGEMENTS

We are grateful to the Radio Times
Hulton Picture Library for permission
to reproduce the photographs on the
front cover and page 4.

ISBN 0 85278 212 8

Printed in Great Britain by
Hart-Talbot Printers Ltd.,
Saffron Walden

Contents

F. D. Roosevelt at his desk

Introduction

This essay does not attempt to describe or analyse in detail either the whole body of New Deal legislation or particular programmes. It is concerned quite simply to consider the general shape of the New Deal in terms of Franklin D. Roosevelt's vision of a just society. In general profile the New Deal is seen as very much the creation of this man who took a lively interest in everything, selected advisers and officials almost deliberately to stimulate creative tension within his administration, and pursued coherent goals by a variety of methods. He seemed to tack with the winds, but the course steered was generally steady. Frequently policies were expedient in timing and in the method of implementation, but within their variegated nature can be found not only a consistency of purpose but a common resort to government intervention. Society was to be restored by the federal government acting in partnership with existing state and local public authorities and with private interest groups, a sort of cooperative federalism that has led one commentator to call the New Deal 'neo-mercantilism democratised'. The term is a clumsy one, but it is suggestive. FDR tried to articulate a middle-way, a centrist position between laissez-faire capitalism and the varying forms of statism that had developed in Europe and elsewhere during the twentieth century.

Roosevelt did not believe in -isms, and there is no easy and generally accepted term to describe the path that he tried to blaze for himself and for the United States. Difficulties of definition almost seem to exceed the problems that Roosevelt himself confronted in the evolution of policy. Liberalism is probably as good a term as any but, despite the efforts of Louis Hartz and others, definitions of liberalism are like pebbles on a beach. Progressivism offers another possibility, but here again philosophical and historical debate has rendered the term of dubious value as a shorthand to understanding what are necessarily complex ideas systems. It is perhaps therefore wise to try to avoid use of a single phrase to encapsulate the New Deal, unless it be that term itself.

This pamphlet is not an exercise in hagiography, an appendix to Carlyle on heroes. Roosevelt is recognised to have been a politician, perhaps indeed a political genius, and he always functioned within a political environment. He was frequently devious, a number of his policies were unsuccessful, and he made mistakes. As McGregor Burns has argued he was part lion, part fox, but he was not a vulgar pragmatist. Whilst always prepared to experiment in terms of method, whilst always able to accept that any administration works within a defined situation that necessarily imposes restraints, and consequently places a premium on accommodation and compromise, expedient and pragmatic policies were directed always towards attaining a set of simple and frequently reiterated goals. These were defined after the beginning of the Second World War as the four freedoms: freedom of speech and of religion, freedom from want and from fear.

They were noble ends, and forty years later they remain for many people remote and seemingly unattainable. Through the New Deal the Roosevelt administration sought to substantiate them in the United States. Its failures are relative.

The New Deal Debate

United States history seems to stimulate impassioned historiography, and the period of the New Deal is no exception. Historical interpretations of the 1930s fall generally within two broad schools: that which stresses the New Deal's discontinuity with the recent American past; and the opposing view that, despite much of its rhetoric, it stayed solidly within an established conservative and capitalist tradition. Much of the debate has been focussed on the question of whether there was or whether there was not a New Deal Revolution.

In his presidential campaign of 1932 Franklin Roosevelt used the word revolution only once. In a short and impromptu speech to Democratic party workers in Indianapolis on 20 October he remarked, as if he wished to disclaim any revolutionary intent, that the election would bring about a revolution, certainly, but of 'the right kind, the only kind of revolution this nation can stand for—a revolution at the ballot box'. However, as the legislative policies of the new Democratic administration began to rush through congress in the spring and summer of 1933 people believed that something new was happening and contemporaries, like many later commentators, began to be pre-occupied with the concept of revolution. Ernest K. Lindley, the distinguished correspondent of the New York *Herald Tribune,* published in 1934 an account of the early months of the Roosevelt administration under the title *The Roosevelt Revolution: First Phase* and concluded that, despite problems of definition, the Roosevelt Revolution was 'democracy, trying to create out of American materials an economic system which will work with reasonable satisfaction to the great majority of citizens'.

Since he wrote, this view of the New Deal as a revolutionary enterprise has been attractive to both advocates and opponents. Thus Carl Degler has written approvingly of 'The Third American Revolution' and the emergence of the 'guarantor state', whilst Edgar Eugene Robinson, in his account of *The Roosevelt Leadership,* is extremely critical of what he believed was an attempt to transform the nature of the American polity. There is also a middle interpretation that sees the New Deal, in William E. Leuchtenburg's judgement, as a radically new departure in American politics but

7

only 'a half-way revolution', a view from which perhaps neither Frank Freidel nor Arthur M. Schlesinger Jr would dissent.

A generation of younger critics of the New Deal, however, discontented with the nature of contemporary American society, have rejected the concept of revolution and see the New Deal as rhetoric without achievement, noteworthy for its failure to achieve significant reforms. Thus Barton J. Bernstein believes that it conserved and protected American capitalism, and that its apparently liberal means were invariably directed towards essentially conservative ends. William A. Williams saw the New Deal as pragmatic to the core and not so much misdirected as undirected. This school shares something in common with frustrated planners like Rexford G. Tugwell, who was disappointed at the failure of the New Deal 'to make America over'.

The debate is not confined to historians. Contemporaries were equally divided. Conservatives of both Republican and Democratic persuasion saw it as an anti-American movement that was subverting the constitution, upsetting the established balance of the federal system, and introducing a degree of what was sometimes called socialism, communism, fascism, or statism in its extension of the role of the federal government and the aggrandizement of the presidency. Typical of this reaction was that of former president Herbert Hoover, who believed that the New Deal would 'undermine and destroy the American system', and 'crack the timbers of the Constitution'. President Franklin D. Roosevelt, the politician so astonishingly and so mistakenly dismissed by the columnist Walter Lippmann in 1932 as 'a pleasant man who, without any important qualifications for the office, would very much like to be President', came to be the man in Dorothy McKay's famous cartoon of 1938 whose name was for many a dirty word. The opposing view is best summarised in the simple words of a tearful black worker as FDR's coffin passed through Washington D.C. in April 1945: 'He hoped me.' Those who had been given hope were always prepared to forgive the imperfections of the New Deal, for it seemed to them to be an attempt to make democracy work.

The President's Vision for America

It is perhaps surprising that the New Deal, unlike Jeffersonian and Jacksonian Democracy, has not been given the name of the president under whose aegis its policies and programmes were initiated and implemented. FDR was, in a very real sense, not only the symbol and personification of his times but also the inspiration behind the many-faceted attack on the problems of depression. As a striking phrase and rallying cry for the faithful 'the New Deal' emerged accidentally. Roosevelt's political confidant Samuel I. Rosenman included it in a draft acceptance speech in 1932, and when Roosevelt electrified the Democratic party National Convention in Chicago on 1 July 1932 with the words: 'I pledge you, I pledge myself, to a new deal for the American people', the phrase was immediately capitalised. It became symbolic of the great expectations projected on to the successful politician by a sorely tried people.

There was no well-defined programme at the time, but rather a set of attitudinal responses towards the problems of government and society out of which legislative policies would emerge. There were also, however, specific achievements in New York State that offered pointers to the probable course of future events. And as the bills came forward, and the acts followed, the New Deal came, in the mind of the President at least, to have form and shape. It was, he said in his radio 'Fireside Chat' on 24 July 1933, not 'just a collection of haphazard schemes, but rather the orderly component parts of a connected and logical whole'.

Before the election, however, 'the New Deal' was instinctively recognised by large sections of the electorate to embody a set of human aspirations and a code of values that, whatever the particular directions set by public policies, whatever anomalies and contradictions policy suggestions seemed to take, would underlie the structure of the attack on social and economic problems. The New Deal was a symbol that inferred a vision of a new America that was not to be a radical break with the past; rather a society in which the original philosophical principles to which the nation had been dedicated since Independence would receive new definition. This would necessarily involve a degree of structural change, despite Bernstein's judgement that the New Deal 'operated within safe elements, far short of Marxism or even of native American radicalism that offered structural critiques and structural solutions'. But it was change that was evolutionary rather than revolutionary, and this fundamental fact about the nature of the New Deal should not be forgotten.

The Background and Apprenticeship of FDR

It is not necessary to make a commitment to psycho-history to believe that the background, character and training of any politician is relevant to the analysis of his public philosophy. Franklin Roosevelt came from a patrician family with estates in the mid-Hudson valley some seventy miles north of New York City. The only son of James and Sara Delano Roosevelt, he was born on 30 January 1882 in the family home at Hyde Park, and his early years were spent in the secure and comfortable world of this almost old-fashioned American aristocracy. The founder of the family, Claes van Rosenvelt had emigrated from Holland to New Amsterdam, now New York, in the 1640s. The Roosevelts prospered in trade and became one among the many 'patroon' landowning families along the Hudson River. Through his maternal stock FDR could claim even earlier arrival in the New World, for they traced their descent from Philippe De La Noye who went to Plymouth plantation in 1621. The Delanos likewise prospered in trade, industry and speculation and, following the European practise that had become equally entrenched in the United States, established themselves as country gentry. Their interests being centred in New York City they also gravitated towards the Hudson valley, but unlike the Roosevelts settled on the less fashionable west bank near Newburgh.

James Roosevelt, after unsuccessful speculations in railroads and in coal, more or less retired to his Hyde Park estates, and it was there that he took his second wife Sara Delano after their marriage in 1880. Sara was the same age as the son of his first marriage, James Roosevelt Roosevelt; she became the dominant partner in the household, particularly in the upbringing of their only child, and was instrumental in sending him to Endicott Peabody's school in Groton, Massachusetts, in 1896. Peabody, an Episcopalian clergyman who believed in the development of Christian character, was a recognisable muscular Christian of the progressive era. He believed above all in service to the community, and in the obligation of the established middle and upper classes to show concern for the dispossessed.

Roosevelt's Early Career

When FDR entered Harvard College in 1900 he carried with him
the humanitarian concerns instilled at Groton but, apart from
occasional visits to a boys club in Boston, pursued the glittering
prizes open to the sons of the American elite. He sought to establish
himself in the undergraduate social clubs, on the athletic fields, in
undergraduate journalism, and as a scholar. He did not excel in any
field but enjoyed himself greatly. After Harvard he moved to New
York, studied law at Columbia and, in 1905, married his distant
cousin Eleanor, niece to President Theodore Roosevelt. Eleanor
was a shy and rather awkward person, her friend and biographer
Joseph Lash calls her the 'outsider'; both parents had died when she
was a child, and her father's alcoholism had not contributed to her
self-confidence. She worked for a while in the settlement house
movement that flourished around the turn of the century, and fell
deeply in love with her dashing cousin FDR. Sara Delano Roosevelt
was initially opposed to the marriage, but despite her dominance
and her devotion to FDR, particularly since James Roosevelt's
death in 1900, he opposed her over the engagement as he was to do
on other issues that he believed to be important. He was never,
however, prepared to remove himself and his wife from her
immediate and continuing influence and Eleanor herself has written,
and her biographer has confirmed, that he was frequently insensitive
to the domestic difficulties presented by the close proximity of a
strong-willed mother-in-law to a devoted but unpractised wife.
Sara built adjoining houses on 65th Street in New York for the two
families, with Hyde Park on the Hudson remaining the family seat.

FDR worked as a Wall Street lawyer for the first years after leaving
law school and then, in 1910, was presented with the oppor-
tunity to enter politics. His branch of the family supported the
Democratic party, unlike the Oyster Bay Roosevelts, and Dutchess
County Democratic leaders urged him to run for the New York
State Assembly. The expected vacancy did not then materialise,
and he was asked to stand for election for the State Senate. In a
Republican district it was thought to be a forlorn hope, but
Roosevelt, accepting the challenge, fought a campaign directed
against 'bossism' and appealed to the widespread progressive
attitudes among the electorate. He canvassed the area in his red
Maxwell touring car, showed himself to be an instinctive politician,
and narrowly won the election. Arrogant, elegant, and a reformer,
his behaviour in the State Senate appalled the party bosses and he
quickly engaged battle with Tammany Hall, the Democratic
organisation in New York City, over the nomination of William F.
Sheehan as United States senator from New York. He and his
friends forced the withdrawal of Sheehan but they themselves had

to accept another Tammany nomination, that of James O'Gorman. Victory, therefore, was only qualified. A pattern was, however, beginning to emerge in Roosevelt's political stance and, despite the superficial political imperative of not making an enemy of Tammany Hall, he had forged an alliance with a broadly definable progressive group. In so doing he perhaps displayed a sensitive political instinct as well as 'virtue' for progressivism was in the ascendancy, and his emerging reform stance coincided in the event with political self-interest.

Emergence in National Politics

In the election of 1912 he won re-election, under the guidance of a new political manager. Louis McHenry Howe was an Albany political journalist, a wizened, asthmatic little man with consider-able political flair who, until his death in 1936, was one of FDR's closest advisers. In the new session of the State legislature Roosevelt began to consolidate his political position as a leading exponent of reform through governmental intervention, but his Albany career was cut short by an invitation to join the Wilson administration as assistant secretary of the Navy. This position was particularly welcome as it had earlier been held by his admired cousin, Theodore Roosevelt, and he was already tempted to see their careers running along similar lines. Impatient as ever, he learned how to move in the wider political world of Washington, loved the ceremonial, and learned a hard political lesson when rebuffed by Tammany and the electorate in a bid for the United States senate in the Democratic primaries of 1914. This experience perhaps helps to explain his later political compromises in the face of entrenched political power. It was a lesson that is reflected in his observation to Samuel Rosenman: that a man may be the greatest statesman the world has ever seen but if he does not have the votes he might·as well be back in the rocking chair on the verandah porch at home. Staying in Washington he worked at his job, gained invaluable experience of the bureaucracy, and demonstrated particular skill in handling labour issues in the dockyards. He became well known, and his availability led him to the Democratic party's vice-presidential nomination at the San Francisco convention of 1920. FDR and the Democratic presidential candidate, Governor James M. Cox of Ohio, fought the campaign on a Wilsonian League of Nations ticket, and lost.

When he left Washington at the end of the Wilson administration FDR returned to business and legal interests in New York City, but in August 1921 contracted polio whilst on holiday at the family summer home at Campobello on the Bay of Fundy. He was paralysed, and never really recovered the use of his legs, despite intensive therapy at Warm Springs, Georgia, but whilst bedridden kept up his political connections. His wife Eleanor and his adviser Louis Howe guided his reading and helped to keep him in touch with politicians and influence brokers. He supported Alfred E. Smith's presidential campaign in 1924 and, in the first major speech since his illness, placed Smith's name in nomination at the Madison Square Garden convention. His role in New York confirmed his standing with rank and file Democrats, and when he named Smith 'the happy warrior of the political battlefield' he added a new phrase to the armoury of party slogans. Decision in the deadlocked convention finally went to a compromise candidate but Roosevelt emerged with enhanced visibility, and then consolidated his position by a deliberate campaign of wooing party leaders throughout the nation in an attempt to strengthen its moderate and progressive wing. Smith remained governor of New York, building what Lubell has called the new Democratic coalition of northern urban, industrial ethnic and labour groups that, together with the 'solid South', might bring victory in 1928. Roosevelt's continuing association with Smith did no harm to his own reputation, and in 1928 he again placed Smith's name in the ring for the presidential nomination, this time successfully. In the national election Smith was heavily defeated by the Republican candidate Herbert Hoover, but Roosevelt, running to succeed Smith as governor of New York, secured a narrow victory in the state. He was now, for the first time, to enjoy executive power, but in a political situation in which he would have to work with a state legislature dominated by the opposition party.

Governor Roosevelt and New York State, the New Deal in Miniature

Roosevelt was re-elected by a landslide in 1930 and there is considerable evidence to suggest that his four years in the Governor's mansion in Albany, years during which the Great Depression struck the nation after the Wall Street Crash of October 1929, forced the consolidation of his progressive attitudes into a set of legislative policies. They led him to formulate clearly his theory of the state and to the conclusion that government must assume responsibility for the health of the economy and the welfare of citizens.

The germs of these developments are to be found in his early political career and, even when expedient political rhetoric is discounted, there can be detected a consistent and visible core of ideas. One of the earliest and most explicit statements of his philosophical position is to be found in a speech made to the People's Forum at Troy, New York, on 3 March 1912. As was his practice, he indulged in an historical preamble that analysed the history of the western world since the Renaissance, portraying it as a struggle for representative government, a search for individual freedom. He concluded that, although generally speaking the liberty of the individual had been accomplished, Utopia had not arrived: the new conditions of the past hundred years had led to a new struggle, a struggle for the liberty of the community rather than for that of the individual. Roosevelt's preoccupation with the liberty of the community meant restriction of individual freedoms for the sake of the public good. The example he gave was taken from the field of conservation, a cause to which he was always devoted. With regard to land and its resources American society had passed beyond the liberty of the individual to do as he pleased with his property, and had found it necessary to check this liberty for the benefit of the freedom of the whole people: 'If the individual's use of his own property affects the whole community, then he must accept regulation by the community of his private property . . .', i.e. particular types of property are particularly affected by the public interest. This attempt to express a form of communitarianism never implied, in Roosevelt's mind, any acceptance of socialism, but rather the development of an indigenous strain in American thought that was not in conflict with the traditions of democratic capitalism. The state was to be the regulator, not the determinant, of economic and social development.

Within America there had always existed a dual tradition that is generally but loosely summarised as Jeffersonianism v. Hamiltonianism. Both groups recognised the legitimacy of state intervention, although they differed in their responses to the problems of federalism. By the 1890s, following the outbursts of populism and the various strands of progressivism, Eric Goldman has been able to find the intellectual paradox of the American system redefined in a struggle between what he calls 'Reform' and 'Conservative' Darwinism. The problem, indeed, came to be one of bringing ideology up to date so that institutions could be brought up to date, so that the country could cope with the demands made upon its political, economic and social infrastructures by twentieth century developments. As FDR said in a speech of 6 July 1928, before the underlying instabilities in the economic system had been exposed: 'We have today side by side an old political order fashioned by a pastoral civilisation and a new social order fashioned by a technical civilisation. The two are maladjusted. Their creative inter-relationship is one of the big tasks ahead of American leadership'. He showed in Albany that he was not averse to picking up this challenge.

Political Problems in the Statehouse

The platform of the New York State Democratic party in 1928, reflecting the leadership of the retiring governor and the general stance of the state party, offered a number of planks on which Roosevelt was fully prepared, ideologically, to stand. The Democrats promised agricultural reform, state control of water power resources, the eight hour day and forty-eight hour week for women and children in industry, consideration of old age pensions, minimum wages for women and children, workingmen's compensation schemes, further prohibitions on the granting of injunctions in industrial disputes, and reforms in the organisation of the state government. In the campaign FDR's political mentor, Louis Howe, worked closely with the secretary of the State Democratic Committee, James Farley, and the two men made a formidable team. Farley had a genius for political craftsmanship, cultivated local officials and exhorted them with highly persuasive and distinctive handwritten green ink letters, a device that was to be invaluable in Roosevelt's presidential campaign in 1932.

In Albany Roosevelt, facing a Republican dominated State legislature, very quickly adopted the technique that he was later to employ in the presidency of appealing over the heads. of the legislature to the people themselves. He used all available forms of communication, including the new medium of radio, which he was probably the first political leader fully to exploit. The genesis of the presidential fire-side chats is to be found in the gubernatorial period, like so much else of the policy and method of the New Deal. Roosevelt saw his job as that of the good manager, who was at the same time sufficiently interested in the people and devoted to their welfare to want constantly to improve their condition.

As is frequently the case, the problems that the Governor had to confront presented themselves. But just as the candidate in 1928 had some choice over the issues he selected for discussion, so did Roosevelt as chief executive of the State of New York influence both the manner and the style of the attack on these problems. A farmer himself, he was profoundly concerned with the plight of the farm community in a state that was one of the major national agricultural producers. New York, like other farm states in the 1920s, was still suffering from the agricultural over-production that had been a characteristic of the world economy since the end of the Great War. Roosevelt appointed as chairman of the State Agricultural Advisory Commission his Hudson valley neighbour, Henry Morgenthau Jr, publisher of *The American Agriculturist* and a leading exponent of the principles of scientific agriculture. In order to try to equalise farm income with that of business and industry the Commission prepared an extensive programme of tax reform to reduce the burden on rural areas that they were ill prepared to meet. It also recommended state assistance to encourage scientific farming and technical studies of cooperative and other marketing techniques. The massive acreage of eroded and worn-out lands was to be tackled through direct state intervention: the Conservation Department was to engage in reforestation programmes that would have the twin advantages of taking depleted lands out of cultivation and rebuilding a land resource base for future exploitation.

The reforestation programme was intimately related to the second major aim of the conservationists: protection and control of water resources. Roosevelt's view was that the state's water power belonged to the people and should be utilised for their benefit. Such utilisation included hydro-electric production and distribution of power to consumers at the lowest possible rate. He confronted the issue in his first inaugural address in 1929, and thereafter worked for state development of the power potential of the St Lawrence. Pre-occupied consistently with the ultimate cost of power to the consumer he also frequently threatened the private utility companies with a state-wide network of state-owned transmission lines unless rates were kept to the minimum. The detailed story of these matters cannot be reviewed here, but as with all other plans and policies it should be noted that Governor Roosevelt was working within a specific political context, and that the Democratic party did not control the state legislature. Frequently, therefore, private interest groups and partisan political opposition inhibited the full development of policy. In relation to the New Deal that was to come, however, it is relevant that during the Albany period FDR was conversant with the ideas of John D. Black of Harvard and M. L. Wilson, the celebrated agricultural economist from Montana State College, leading exponents of the domestic allotment plan which was a direct forerunner of the attempt during the New Deal to curb the problem of over-production by the allocation of acreage quotas.

Governor Roosevelt's Reactions to the Great Depression

The problems of other sectors of the economy had been largely concealed by the prosperity of the New Economic Era of the Twenties, but once the crash came and the general depression deepened these also demanded attention. Two of the most publicised symbols of the collapse are the pathetic apple sellers on the streets of New York and the Hoovervilles that sprang up around many cities, shanty towns of tar paper and boxes that housed the homeless and the jobless. Distress was widespread and by February 1933 Edmund Wilson could report in the *New Republic* that 'there is not a garbage-dump in Chicago which is not diligently haunted by the hungry. Last summer in the hot weather when the smell was sickening and the flies were thick, there were a hundred people a day coming to one of the dumps . . . (A) widow who used to do housework and laundry, but now had no work at all, fed herself and her fourteen-year-old son on garbage. Before she picked up the meat, she would always take off her glasses so that she couldn't see the maggots'.

President Hoover was a great and good man, but although he modified his traditional attitudes under pressure of adversity, and policies such as establishment of the Reconstruction Finance Corporation helped to create an institutional framework within which, after 4 March 1933, President Roosevelt would work, he clung to the remnants of the traditional American ideology of individualism and laissez-faire. He continued to believe in private charity, which was 'the obligation of the strong to the weak', and that 'works of charity are the tests of spiritual development of men and women and communities'. He suggested that if federal aid were instituted, 'we have not only impaired something infinitely valuable in the life of the American people but have struck at the roots of self-government'. However, the facts were that in Illinois, for example, the Red Cross could by 1931 provide only seventy-five cents a week to feed hungry families. The situation had developed far beyond the ability of private charity to cope. The President did not have an instinct for public relations, was unfortunately photographed feeding his dog at a time when people were starving, and his Secretary of War, Patrick Hurley, was recorded as advising that restaurants scrape the scraps left by diners into five gallon cans for distribution to the poor.

The depression produced a folk art in music, such as 'Breadline Blues' and many others that came to embody the different popular perceptions of Hoover and Roosevelt. The difference is painfully presented after Roosevelt's inauguration in the haunting refrain of 'White House Blues': 'Look here, Mr Hoover, it's see what you done, You went off a fishin' let the country go to ruin, Now he's gone, I'm glad he's gone! Roosevelt's in the White House, doing his best, While old Hoover is layin around and rest, Now he's gone (doghide), I'm glad he's gone'. Even before the 1932 election the contrast between the attitudes of the administration in Washington and those of the New York state government in the person of Roosevelt were startling. The Governor, in calling for state aid to the unemployed in 1931, stated that such help should be given 'not as a matter of charity, but as a matter of social duty'. It seems impossible to avoid the conclusion that for Hoover, despite his compassion, the relationship between government and society was one in which the role of the government should be minimal and remote from the individual citizen. Society was a collection of individuals who should help themselves and help each other. Roosevelt on the other hand was primarily interested in government, and in principles of government, for the sake of those governed. The state existed for the direct benefit of its citizens: principles should therefore be thrown out of the window whenever the situation demanded a change of policy.

As Bernard Bellush has emphasised in his study of the governorship period, Roosevelt did not formulate theories or policies in advance of the need for action and he, like President Hoover, believed at first that the depression would be short lived. However, once the need for action impressed itself he was prepared to confront particular problems by any and all available means. He set up a Committee on Stabilization of Industry for the Prevention of Unemployment, expanded the activities of the Department of Public Works, and by 1931 had persuaded the Republican dominated state legislature to establish a Temporary Emergency Relief Administration with an appropriation of $20,000,000 for both home and work relief. TERA, with an initial life of one year, was later extended.

As the depression deepened the plight of the old and the sick as well as that of the unemployed became acute. As early as the campaign of 1928 Roosevelt had urged the establishment of a contributory pension scheme and this was later widened to include unemployment insurance. Awareness of the fact that problems transcended state boundaries led the Governor to press the issue upon his fellow governors at the national and regional governors' conferences, and New York State initiatives were crucial in leading to the establishment of the Interstate Commission for the Study of Unemployment Insurance that first met in May 1931. The complexity of the issues involved, together with their political implications, delayed positive action, but seeds had been planted that were to bear fruit in the federal Social Security Act of 1935.

Associated with this was Roosevelt's concern with workingmen's compensation, conditions of work for women and children, particularly in the 'sweatshops', use of the injunction in labour disputes, minimum wages and maximum hours. The Governor did not go as far on any issue as organised labour wanted, but his ideas and his commitments were becoming clarified. A not unimportant or irrelevant by-product was consolidation of the developing alliance of the labour movement with the Democratic Party.

A Pragmatic Ideology for the New Deal?

The approach throughout was pragmatic. The emphasis placed in the Oglethorpe speech in the 1932 presidential campaign on the need for 'bold, persistent experimentation' was in tune with the Governor's observation a year earlier that 'the new factors in our lives is (sic) the result of experimentation and it is therefore only logical and not radical to insist that through experimentation also we must solve the social and economic difficulties of the present'.

The positive steps taken by the state administration in his first term were outlined by Roosevelt in a letter to Senator Robert F. Wagner of 9 September 1930, but the series of practical measures was not divorced from a philosophy of government. This was best expressed in a message to the state legislature in Albany on 28 August 1931, an impressive message in context and one which must have both astounded and enraged sections of his audience. He threw out the rhetorical question 'What is the State?', and then gave his own answer: 'It is the duly constituted representatives of an organised society of human beings, created by them for their mutual protection and well-being. "The State" or "The Government" is but the machinery through which such mutual aid and protection are achieved . . . Our Government is not the master but the creature of the people. The duty of the State towards its citizens is the duty of the servant to its master. The people have created it; the people by common consent, permit its continued existence.'

'One of these duties of the State is that of caring for those of its citizens who find themselves the victims of such adverse circumstances as makes them unable to obtain even the necessities for mere existence without the aid of others. That responsibility is recognised by every civilised Nation . . .'

. . . 'upon the State falls the duty of protecting and sustaining those of its citizens who, through no fault of their own, find themselves in their old age unable to maintain life.'

'But the same rule applies to other conditions. In broad terms I assert that modern society, acting through its Government, owes the definite obligation to prevent the starvation or the dire want of any of its fellow men and women who try to maintain themselves but cannot.'

Later in this address Roosevelt committed himself to the extension of government aid as a matter of social duty rather than charity. In the speech as a whole Roosevelt was not only trying to articulate his concept of the state as regulator, but was throwing down the gauntlet before the Republican opposition. His views were, however, philosophically consistent with the ideas expressed in the Troy speech of 1912. They embraced Theodore Roosevelt's concept of the role of the state as a balancing force in society designed to produce equilibrium between its component parts in the public interest, and suggested some familiarity with Herbert Croly's *The Promise of American Life* (1909). This famous progressive document saw the state not as an abstract entity but rather as something that lives and grows by what it does. Pragmatism has been called the American philosophy, and it may indeed offer a key towards unravelling the complexity of a New Deal that is often said to be indefinable.

Misconceptions of the nature of pragmatism have fuelled interpretations of the New Deal as merely a set of expedient responses to socio-economic and political pressures, as reflexes that were not sustained by over-reaching aims. But philosophically pragmatism should not be simply equated with expediency. It neither regards action as an end in itself nor presumes that any means are justified if they work. The pragmatist relates value and meaning to specific contexts and insists that values are themselves facts. Such thinking involves a degree of objective relativism that leads to acceptance of fallibilism and probabilism, and the taking of risks in a form of experimentalism that is far removed from unprincipled opportunism. Patterns are not pre-determined, and there is a continuum of means and ends, so that the ends sought are inevitably influenced by the means employed: means therefore determine ends just as much as ends determine means. The pragmatist is also a meliorist and an incrementalist who in his search for improvements rejects utopian solutions. The best is therefore the enemy of the better, and theoretical social planning is rejected in favour of progressive, incremental change that starts from acceptance of the complex structures of society and the existence of established interest groups.

Emphasis on individualism does not therefore identify the individual as a lonely person struggling to survive in a Darwinian environment. He is an individual who lives in society, and individual effort is not the only instrumentality of social change; collective means are also called for in a complex social order. Acceptance of this sort of collectivism, however, in the sense in which Roosevelt used the concept of the community in the Troy speech, did not mean adherence to the type of collectivism that men such as Rexford G. Tugwell advocated. Rex Tugwell's qualified disenchantment with the New Deal was a measure of the extent to which the 'planners' were misled in their belief that Roosevelt could be led to adopt theoretical collectivist solutions for the problems of depression.

Pragmatism and Planning

Certainly Roosevelt frequently spoke of planning. In his acceptance speech to the Democratic national convention in Chicago on 2 July 1932 he said that the Democratic party had to be the party of 'Liberal thought, of planned action'. In his First Inaugural he spoke of the need for national planning. In the message to congress of 10 April 1933 in which he proposed setting up a Tennessee Valley Authority he spoke of the need to 'extend planning to a wider field, in this instance comprehending in one great project many States directly concerned with the basin of one of our greatest rivers'. In his radio address on the recovery programme delivered on 24 July 1933 he spoke of 'the fundamentals of this planning for national recovery', and declared that the policies of the 100 Days were not just random, but together formed a comprehensive programme. This is persuasive if consistency of aim and inclusive concern for all interests are not confused with a search for consistent methods of attaining goals.

The pragmatist is also a pluralist, accepting that differences between individuals, and between the groups into which they naturally coalesce, are intrinsic to their individuality. While collectivist theories usually embrace holistic philosophies, in an individualistic and hence pluralistic society which is at the same time democratic the democratic element is the method of arriving at social policy, a method of decision-making through an agreed process of rational choice. Laws are not immutable, aims are not simply material. As Roosevelt insisted in the acceptance speech, work and security are more than words and facts, they are spiritual values. 'Economic laws are not made by nature. They are made by human beings'; hence the emphasis in the Oglethorpe speech on bold persistent experimentation. The means are not sacred although the goals are; and these goals are the 'social values more noble than mere monetary profit' of the First Inaugural.

Such ideas infuse what has been called one of the most complete statements that Roosevelt made of his political philosophy: the speech to the Commonwealth Club of San Francisco on 23 September 1932 at the height of the presidential campaign. After his customary historical preamble about the evolution of western civilisation, Roosevelt declared that 'the day of enlightened administration has come' and that the essential role of government was to help to bring about 'an economic declaration of rights, an economic constitutional order'. The basis of this order was to be recognition that man had certain basic rights. These rights were coherently defined as the right to life and a comfortable living; the right to property and hence to the security of savings; the right to liberty— which means the right to 'read, to think, to speak, to choose and live a mode of life'. In order to defend these rights the government must use its countervailing power to check the excesses of particular interest groups whose actions deprive others of their rights. The government, in fulfilling its duty to protect the public interest, must intervene as a balancing force in the attempt to maintain equilibrium.

The Moderating Influence of Interest Group Politics

Although historians such as James McGregor Burns have been tempted into cynicism when writing about 'the politics of broker leadership', it is not easy to see how policies of aggressive confrontation with entrenched socio-economic groups would have produced more effective counter-depression measures than those that were tried. Moreover Roosevelt was not averse to political challenge, not restrained in the language of confrontation when it seemed appropriate. In his First Inaugural Address he spoke of the money changers who had 'fled from their high seats in the temples of our civilization', and declared that the temple had been restored to the ancient truths; in his speech of acceptance of nomination for a second term, at the Democratic convention in Philadelphia in 1936, he attacked the economic royalists who practised economic slavery. This was politics; it was also policy. But he firmly believed that in both the formulation and implementation of policy regard had to be paid to the existing structures of society and to the influence and power of established interests. Such interests not only exercised a socio-economic role; they were also represented in both the federal and the state legislatures. Their influence can therefore be detected in the particular policies of the New Deal, for Roosevelt was not prepared to commit political suicide, but it is also true that he did not want radically to redefine the nature of American civilisation. Roosevelt never entirely seized the initiative, and it is doubtful that he ever wanted to do so; his strength lay in his ability to suggest leadership, his instinctive manipulative skills, his recognition of the power of consensus politics, his belief in the dignity and rights of the common man, his resiliant and confident temperament, and his innate commitment to democracy which always qualified any temptation to enlarge the power of the state beyond what he considered to be the limits imposed by the democratic tradition.

The essence of his programme was to give 'the forgotten man at the bottom of the economic pyramid' a fair share of the natural abundance of society, and 'the objective of government . . . (was) to provide at least as much assistance to the little fellow as it is now giving to the large banks and corporations'.

Some scholars, such as Arthur Ekirch in *Ideologies and Utopias*, have characterised the New Deal as representing the emergence of 'a new public philosophy'. It was not in its elements new, but the existence and impact of the depression demanded action and provided opportunity for the introduction of measures that were not in themselves strangers to the American tradition but which all came together for the first time. The impact of the New Deal lies in the sum of its parts.

In 1935 Walter Lippmann published *The Good Society*, a book which, as Henry Steele Commager states in *The American Mind*, repudiated the 'doctrines of both the extreme right and the extreme left'. . . but levelled its most deadly 'attack against that peversion of classical economics which masqueraded as liberalism'. Freedom in society was not the absence of governmental planning or governmental controls but, in Locke's words, to have a standing law to live by. Rejecting both rugged individualism and collectivism, Lippmann argued the case for responsible state intervention in the social and economic life of the nation in order to equalise opportunity, destroy special privilege and level artificial barriers. Stressing the fact that in the long run the means determine the ends, he disapproved of some of the methods of the New Deal because they suggested administrative fiat. Nevertheless he was trying to define a middle way between socialism and laissez-faire individualism that, in its political agenda, Commager argues, was akin to that of the New Deal. The search for a New Deal ideology must be made in this middle ground between the conflicting isms. When questioned about his political philosophy Roosevelt, on one famous occasion, replied simply that he was a Christian and a democrat; this was the response of an intelligent but non–intellectual man accustomed to express his ideas in homely metaphor and unadorned phrase. He liked to listen to intellectuals and talk with politicians. The latter understood him; the former were frequently puzzled, including John Maynard Keynes who was disappointed that a man who seemed to be following Keynesian policies could apparently be economically illiterate. Roosevelt was, moreover, said Keynes, like a 'big fluffy pillow. He bears the imprint of the last person who sat on him'. The President did have an absorbent mind, and ideas came from many sources, but sometimes his amiable receptivity was the device consciously developed by a man who had lost the use of his legs. He could not stand to terminate an interview, but he could send his caller on his way believing that his case had been well put.

The New Deal in Action

The New Deal has seemed to many like a thick alphabet soup in which everyone could find his initials. An emergency session of congress was convened on 9th March 1933 and thus began the famous 100 Days during which a spate of legislation and executive proclamations poured forth and gave some body to the promise of the New Deal. Some were well-considered, others instant responses to demanding problems, for 'action, action now' was important in order to restore confidence. The *New York Times* columnist Anne O'Hare McCormick wrote on 7 May 1933: 'Wherever you go in Washington today you come upon crowds of people . . . Always they are eager, anxious; always they are talking . . . You feel the stir of movement, of adventure, even of elation. You never before saw in Washington so much government, or so much animation in government. Everybody in the administration is having the time of his life . . . They are going somewhere, that is plain, and with such momentum and elan that they take the world in the same stride with which they set about reconstructing agriculture, reflating the currency, reforming the structure of business and industry'.

The 'First' and 'Second' New Deals

Ever since Basil Rauch's early study of the New Deal it has been customary to divide the period into two phases, the first from 1933 to 1934, and a second from 1935 to 1938. The concept of the two New Deals is posited on the belief that the first New Deal was preoccupied with recovery, the second with reform, and it has also been suggested that the reform phase only came as a consequence of what McGregor Burns has called the 'thunder on the left'; *i.e.* that Roosevelt, as always bowing to political pressure and suffused with political ambition, was forced into a reform stance by pressures from the 'left' that he had to satisfy in order to preserve his political position as the 1936 elections approached. The argument here is that the New Deal is better seen as a whole. Reform elements are built into the early 'recovery' policies, and recovery policies are integral to the 'reform' phase.

The first measure was proclamation of a national bank holiday to stop the run on banks; and on the first of the Hundred Days the Emergency Banking Act extended federal controls over the banking system and provided for the opening of 'sound' banks under licence from the Treasury Department. This measure to instil confidence was followed by an Economy Act that, according to prevailing economic orthodoxy, sought to bring the 'normal' expenditures of the federal government into balance with income. Extra revenue was, however, expected as a consequence of the Beer-Wine Revenue Act, and budget deficits on 'abnormal' expenditure were anticipated. The Civilian Conservation Corps was established as a direct response to unemployment, and 250,000 jobs on reforestation and conservation projects were envisaged for unemployed males between the ages of 18 and 25. Work camps were established and the programme was one of the successes of the New Deal: by the time it ended in 1941 over 2 million jobs had been provided. The Federal Emergency Relief Act, with an appropriation of 500 million dollars, represented the translation to national level of New York State's TERA, and embodied a principle that was characteristic of much of the New Deal legislation. Despite critics' charges, there was no deliberate attempt during the 1930s to transform the American polity by gross enlargement of federal authority over the states. The guiding principle was federal-state cooperation, with the federal government offering funds to participating authorities on a matching basis. The New Deal developed pragmatically a type of cooperative federalism instead of trying to take the alternative course of superimposed nationalism.

The Agricultural Adjustment Act of 12 May 1933 was the first major attack on agricultural distress. Adopting many of the ideas of the farm lobbies of the 1920s the act sought to control the problem of over-production and low farm prices by curtailing production through acreage reductions on a quota basis. Decisions were made locally, usually on a county basis, and the programme was therefore open to self-interested manipulation by dominant local groups but this was inevitable. Total centralisation was alien to the New Deal; it was also impossible due to the absence of a developed federal bureaucracy to administer policy in detail. The concept of 'parity' prices for farmers was built into the Act and a complicated system of subsidy was developed for particular sectors of agriculture. The act establishing the Tennessee Valley Authority on 18 May 1933 attacked not only agricultural depression in the region but another major issue that was of prime importance for Roosevelt: the development of public power. Structurally, and in terms of its lasting success, it is one of the most important pieces of legislation that came out of the 100 Days. It envisaged regional planning of the entire Tennessee Valley area to control the river and its tributaries, restore eroded lands, encourage scientific farming and, as a by-product, produce large quantities of power that would be sold as cheaply as possible to provide a 'yardstick' for private utility companies. The concept of regional planning to relieve problems that transcend traditional political boundaries was one that Roosevelt had urged on the governors' conferences, and one that he later sought, unsuccessfully, to extend beyond TVA.

In order to reflate, Roosevelt took the country off the gold standard. The Federal Securities Act, strengthened and expanded by the establishment in 1934 of the Securities and Exchange Commission, introduced regulation of the securities market. To protect home mortgages a Home Owners Loan Corporation was established, and to protect small bank deposits the Federal Bank Deposit Insurance Corporation was set up. Farm Credits were channelled through the FCA. The National Employment System Act embodied the principle of federal-state co-operation, and attack on the major problem of industrial depression was launched in the clumsy omnibus bill that became the National Industrial Recovery Act of 16 June 1933. Seeking to revive industrial activity and reduce unemployment the act contained two major titles. The first adopted elements of the old trade association idea and provided for the drafting of codes of fair competition that sought to regulate prices, output, hours of work and levels of wages. The famous section 7(a) that came to be called 'labour's charter' guaranteed to labour the right to organise and to bargain collectively through representatives of their own choosing. Under the act a National Labor Board was established to protect these rights. Title 11 of the Act authorised an appropriation of 3.3 billion dollars for the creation of public works projects. These were run by a Public Works Administration under the direction of the Secretary of the Interior, Harold Ickes, a crusty old progressive from Chicago. Under Ickes' careful management the pump priming activities of PWA were slow to get off the ground and later in the year the Civil Works Administration was created to provide work on short term projects that could be quickly implemented. This, under Roosevelt's crony Harry Hopkins, a former social worker from New York, quickly spent almost one billion dollars on work projects for the unemployed.

There were many other programmes, many other alphabetical agencies. In 1934 came the Farm Mortgage Refinancing Act, the Civil Works Emergency Relief Act, the Crop Loan Act, the Jones-Connally Farm Relief Act, the Home Owners Loan Act, the Municipal Bankruptcy Act, the Federal Farm Bankruptcy Act, the National Housing Act. Under the Emergency Relief Appropriation Act of 1935 Hopkins was placed in charge of the Works Progress Administration that put millions of people to work. Some called them leaf-raking projects but almost every American city has WPA built pavements, post-offices, bridges, parks etc. Writers, artists and musicians were not forgotten and each sector found a federal programme that put people to work, using their natural skills.

In 1935 the Resettlement Administration under Rexford Tugwell sought to re-establish people on self-sufficient farms or subsistence homesteads; the Rural Electrification Agency of the same year literally brought light and electric power to rural America. The National Labor Relations Act and the Social Security Act of 1935 were landmarks in the evolution of the American labor movement and in the introduction of a recognisably 'modern' social security system. The Soil Conservation and Domestic Allotment Act of 1936 and the second Triple A of 1938 advanced the policy of conserving that most permanent and valuable natural resource, land, and continued the attack on rural poverty. Successive Revenue Acts extended the principle of the graduated income tax in the attempt 'to prevent an unjust concentration of wealth and economic power'.

This simple catalogue of legislation does little justice to the complexity of the problems confronted by the New Deal; nor does it consider the frailty, the ineffectiveness and the confusions of many of the programmes. Judicious use of the bibliography will expose these matters and challenge the reader. Steinbeck has immortalised the problems of the Okies in *The Grapes of Wrath,* and any set of statistical tables will reveal the extent to which the Roosevelt administration failed to solve the economic problems of the United States in the third decade of the twentieth century. It was only when, in Roosevelt's phrase, Dr New Deal was replaced by Dr Win-the-War that the economy was fully restored. It would be unwise, however, to scurry from over-optimistic faith in the New Deal to excessive and hypercritical pessimism about its achievements, even in economic terms. Jim Potter has recently concluded that 'the recovery of the years 1933-7 was almost as great as the expansion of 1922-9'; and that 'if it is argued . . . that the expansion of the twenties was indeed remarkable, then *ipso facto* a standard has already been set against which to measure the achievement of the thirties'.

This essay does not explore the economic successes and failures of the New Deal and it has ignored many important and central features of the period. Nothing has been written about the struggle of labour to organise, of the battles fought in the steel and automobile industries. Nothing has been written about the opposition to Roosevelt through the Liberty League, the Republican Party, or indeed from elements within his own Democratic Party. Nothing has been written about the New Deal in the States, although the work of James Patterson and his followers has shown the importance of microstudies; the complexity of the continental nation with its federal system was reflected in the complexity of the New Deal in operational terms. There has been no analysis of that phenomenon of the 1932 campaign and of the early New Deal, the Brains Trust; and leading personalities have been referred to only briefly, if at all. Frances Perkins, the first woman cabinet member, served as Secretary of Labor from 1933 until the end in 1945, knew Roosevelt as well as any man and would have to dominate detailed analysis of those parts of the New Deal that fell within her jurisdiction. Huey Long, the Louisiana Kingfish who threatened political challenge to Roosevelt, Dr Charles Townsend and his revolving old age pension plan, Upton Sinclair and his EPIC campaign in California, Father Coughlin of the Shrine of the Little Flower, these and other phenomena have been ignored. The problems of Black Americans have not been noticed. Attention has been focussed on the personality and goals of the President himself, in an attempt to suggest that, despite many of its apparent contradictions, there was an overall shape to the New Deal that makes the period highly significant in the growth of a mixed, welfare economy in the United States. There is, however, one issue involving FDR that forms a necessary coda to this discussion.

Roosevelt the Revolutionary?

In one significant respect FDR did come to believe that the American system should be radically changed to enable government, expressing the will of the people, to govern according to that will without let or hindrance. In his study of *The Imperial Presidency* Arthur M. Schlesinger rightly notes that Roosevelt preferred to base his actions on congressional legislation rather than on executive privilege, and that in the First Inaugural FDR warned of his intention of asking congress for broad executive power to wage war against the emergency. This he did, and congress gave him great delegated power, as in the NIRA, to effect the policies generally defined by the legislature. This delegation, however, was not permanent but was given for a maximum of two years, and it was surrounded by what the congress believed to be sufficient safeguards. The 'flow of power to the presidency' was therefore contained, and much of the New Deal was founded on this partnership between the two elected branches of the federal government. Challenge from the third and non-elected branch, however, led Roosevelt into a curiously radical posture.

The New Deal and the Supreme Court

In the American system the nine men of the Supreme Court, none of whom was as yet a Roosevelt appointee, held the power to determine the constitutionality of legislation, and hence the constitutionality of the New Deal. There is continuing debate at all periods about the extent to which the personal, political, social, and economic beliefs of individual justices influence their voting patterns, and the issue is unlikely to be resolved. When New Deal legislation began to arrive before the Court its decisions are not easy to classify. A number of measures, including TVA, which was central to the recovery and reform programme as a whole, were sustained by the Court, but others, such as the NIRA and the AAA, were declared to be unconstitutional. In the Schechter case involving the NIRA the Court held that there had been an unconstitutional delegation by the congress to the executive of what was essentially legislative power, and that this was unconstitutional for 'extraordinary conditions do not create or enlarge constitutional power'. In a concurring opinion Justice Cardozo expressed it succinctly: 'the delegated power of legislation . . . is not canalized within banks that keep it from overflowing. It is unconfined and vagrant'. In the case of *US v Butler* that concerned the Triple A Justice Roberts wrote the majority opinion and had no doubt about the unconstitutionality of the Act, but emphasised that the Court 'neither approves nor condemns any legislative policy', merely decides on narrower issues of constitutionality. In a dissenting opinion, however, Justice Stone argued a theory of judicial restraint, and declared that 'for the removal of unwise laws from the statute books appeal lies not to the courts but to the ballot and to the processes of democratic government'.

Although there is reason to believe that the administration had never been totally convinced of the constitutionality of the two acts in question, and had been content to let the matter be ultimately resolved in the courts, Roosevelt's response was immediate. He declared that the country was in danger of being cast back into 'the horse and buggy' age, and accepted what he saw to be direct challenge to the authority of the executive–legislative partnership. This led him to articulate a new political concept and to fight the two most destructive political battles of his career: the Court 'packing plan' and direct intervention in the Democratic primary elections in 1938. He was prepared to accommodate himself to political challenge from elected legislatures, but not to what he saw as political challenge from an appointive court, and he came to expound a theory of majoritarian democracy that was alien to the American tradition and posited a party structure defined by ideological difference.

As has been suggested, FDR had long been concerned to strengthen the progressive elements within the Democratic coalition. In his acceptance speech in 1932 he told the assembled delegates that 'ours must be a Party of Liberal thought, of planned action, of enlightened international outlook, and of the greatest good to the greatest number of our citizens', and the following month he declared to Rex Tugwell: 'I'll be in the White House for eight years. When those years are over, there'll be a Progressive party. It may not be Democratic, but it will be Progressive'. This liberal Democratic and Progressive party would be based on the people and would, he believed, represent the majority will of the nation.

He saw his landslide victory in 1936 as evidence of a great popular mandate for the New Deal, as well as for himself, and believed that the problem had become one of making democracy work, and of preventing the majority on the Supreme Court from 'legislating on the desirability rather than the constitutionality of laws'. This led him in January 1937 to introduce legislation into the new congress that would increase the size of the Supreme Court in a complex scheme that became known as the Court Packing Plan. As he later wrote in the introduction to the 1937 volume of *The Public Papers*: 'For two decades the Supreme Court of the United States had been successfully thwarting the common will of the overwhelming majority of the American people; and had been diverting the functions and philosophy of government into channels which ran counter to the thought and objectives of progressive opinions throughout the modern civilised world'. What he called 'the dead hand of the Court' was preventing government action in pursuit of valid socio-economic objectives.

The Court Packing Plan failed, but a change seemed to come about in the pattern of the Court's opinions. Whether or not this was so, and whether or not the Supreme Court so acted to save itself—the famous 'switch in time saves nine'—Roosevelt believed that he had won the battle and that therefore 'the federal government now has the undisputed powers which had always been intended for it by the framers of the Constitution . . . Democracy proved again that it had within it the power to function'. FDR was therefore not claiming a revolutionary success, but rather fulfilment of the intentions of Founding Fathers who had drafted an organic not a static constitution. It is clear, however, that he was asserting the supremacy of the collective will of the executive and legislative branches, whose acts should normally be sustained by the Court, and that legislation should be denied only as an exceptional and last resort.

The New Deal and 'Liberal Democracy'

In 1938 came the next step towards updating the political system. If not revolutionary it was certainly a radical challenge to the existing two party system, which was traditionally based on the concept of party as a coalition of interests in a pluralistic society. Roosevelt, however, consistent with his statements to Tugwell in 1932, moved towards re-building the Democratic party on ideological lines. The title of the 1938 volume of *The Public Papers* is revealing: *The Continuing Struggle for Liberalism*. He apparently saw it as his duty to make his party the truly liberal party of America, and he defined a liberal party as one 'which believes that, as new conditions and problems arise beyond the power of men and women to meet as individuals, it becomes the duty of Government itself to find new remedies with which to meet them. The liberal party insists that the Government has the definite duty to use all its power and resources to meet new social problems with new social controls— to ensure to the average person the right to his own economic and political life, liberty, and the pursuit of happiness'. The conservative party, implicitly the Republicans, is the negative party that rejects government intervention.

In order to try to make the Democratic party more liberal Roosevelt intervened in the Democratic primary elections of 1938 to try to defeat candidates opposed to progressive and liberal government. The theme was stated in Georgia and Maryland, and in an extended national radio address on electing liberals to public office that he called 'The Fight for Social Justice and Economic Democracy'. Despite the application of considerable pressure Roosevelt almost completely failed in his attempt to purge conservative Democrats and suffered one of his greatest political defeats. Was the attempt to reconstruct the Democratic Party an act of political courage, or an egotistic and grandiloquent response to the landslide victory in 1936? His enemies had always seen power-hungriness behind his personal charm and democratic rhetoric. Certainly his political antennae seemed to have been bent, perhaps by the 1936 victory, perhaps as a result of the death of Louis Howe and other changes in the ranks of his close advisers. Had he been successful in subordinating the Court and transforming the party there would indeed have been a Roosevelt Revolution of far-reaching consequences.

Conclusion

The Roosevelt presidency contained inherently revolutionary tendencies in its assumption that government must accept a degree of direct responsibility for the domestic security of the American citizen. It was certainly characterised by an enlargement of the power and influence of the White House, by the establishment of an executive bureaucracy, and by the personalisation of policy, but it was very different from what Arthur Schlesinger Jr has called the tendency towards a revolutionary presidency in the Nixon period. Nixon's was a presidency increasingly insulated and isolated from the people, and suspicious of the people. Roosevelt drew his strength from the people, had a deep faith in their instinctive wisdom, and wooed them with his fireside chats, his public tours, and his folksiness at Hyde Park and Warm Springs. The New Deal was rooted in progressive democracy; this led to belief that government intervention in the economy, according to the expressed will of the sovereign people, was necessary in the complex conditions of the advanced industrial state. The projected system envisaged executive and legislature working in harmony to carry out the people's mandate, and on the occasions when the congress insisted on qualifying presidential policies Roosevelt would invariably accommodate himself to their wishes. When the people spoke in the primaries of 1938 he also accepted their verdict with good grace.

What he sought to achieve in his attack on 'hear-nothing, see-nothing, do-nothing Government' was not the introduction of rigid state control; the emphasis was always on cooperation not compulsion. For this reason, from the beginning, there was a rejection of state intervention based on concepts of efficiency. Roosevelt's view of the 'Big Job' in an interview in 1932 was that it was 'more than an engineering job, efficient or inefficient'. Seeing the presidency as 'pre-eminently a place of moral leadership' Roosevelt was prepared to deploy the powers of government within a democratic system that itself suggested definition of a middle way. He tried to encapsulate what was to be the nature of the New Deal in one of his simple metaphors: 'Say the New Deal is a tree which, as it grows, continually produces rot and dead wood. The radical says: "Cut it down." The conservative says: "Don't touch it." The liberal compromises: "Let's prune, so that we lose neither the old trunk nor the new branches." This campaign is waged to teach the country to march upon its appointed course, the way of change, in an orderly march, avoiding alike the revolution of radicalism and the revolution of conservatism.' Adolf Berle sensed the nature of this 'difficult course of moderation' in an essay 'The Social Economics of the New Deal' in October 1933. Donald Richberg summarised the objective in terms of the NRA as 'seeking to establish a half-way house of democratic cooperation for the common good, midway between the anarchy of unplanned, unregulated industrialism and the tyranny of State control of industry.'

This middle way had its own vision. It was not, as Roosevelt told the Young Democrats in 1935, the old 'dream of the golden ladder—each individual for himself', but a different dream that emphasised security for the individual in the context of a secure society. This seems a coherent goal for a man who was, in Rosenman's phrase, 'a confirmed and relentless liberal'. Roosevelt was not in his heart a revolutionary but he was committed to the regeneration of American society. He believed that the promise of American life could only be fulfilled, and liberty prevail, if democratic constraints were imposed on the capitalist system and government became the conscience of the people.

By 1939 questions of conscience were increasingly dominated by foreign rather than domestic concerns. A counter-point to the domestic political debates of the 1930s had been the issue of what should be the role of the United States in world affairs. Arguments between isolationists and inter-nationalists had confused normal political alliances and obscured the emergence of an agreed liberal consensus as the Italian conquest of Abyssinia, the Spanish Civil War, and the struggle of Japan and China in the Far East challenged what many believed to be an American tradition of neutrality. When war broke out in Europe in 1939 foreign policy questions came to dominate the internal United States political process as Roosevelt moved towards what later came to be called the 'arsenal of democracy' concept.

As an 'active non-belligerent' American policies toward the European war, in conjunction with the response of the United States to Japan in the Far East, produced an alignment with the European democracies and with China that made Pearl Harbor if not inevitable at least calculable. After December 1941, with the coming of war prosperity, some New Deal programmes became unnecessary, some were cancelled, others became transformed by the new circumstances. But in 1945 enough of the New Deal remained as part of the foundations of the American system of government and society to give heart to later Democratic presidents who sought to build their own forms of the good society.

Although the tendency towards 'big government' continued to be reviled by many Republicans and conservative Democrats, much of what had once been divisive was now accepted as legitimate. That the role of government in society is once again under question should be no surprise, for it is the tragedy of liberalism that particular forms quickly become old fashioned at times of great change.

Bibliography

The literature on the New Deal is immense. The selection listed here is but a small sample of works that are generally available, often in paperback, and that relate to the themes discussed in the preceding essay. Each title is given only once, in the section to which it has particular relevance, but most will have more general reference. Editions cited are those used by the writer.

The best single monograph remains William E. Leuchtenburg: *Franklin D. Roosevelt and the New Deal 1932-1940* (N.Y., 1963); another excellent one volume study is James McGregor Burns: *Roosevelt: The Lion and The Fox* (N.Y., 1956).

The two classic but unfinished biographies are Frank Freidel: *Franklin D. Roosevelt* (4 vols Boston, 1952-73), and Arthur M. Schlesinger, Jr: *The Age of Roosevelt* (3 vols Boston, 1957-60).

A recent composite study incorporating the most recent scholarship is John Braeman, Robert H. Bremner and David Brody eds: *The New Deal* (2 vols Columbus, Ohio, 1975).

Indispensable to the study of FDR and the New Deal are Samuel I. Rosenman ed: *The Public Papers and Addresses of Franklin D. Roosevelt 1928-1936* (5 vols N.Y., 1938) and *1937-1940* (4 vols N.Y., 1941).

Introduction

A useful collection of commentaries is Bernard Sternsher ed.: *The New Deal, Doctrines and Democracy* (Boston, 1966); see also Howard Zinn ed.: *New Deal Thought* (Indianapolis, 1966), Paul Conkin: *The New Deal* (N.Y., 1967) and John Major ed.: *The New Deal* (London, 1968). Louis Hartz discusses liberalism in *The Liberal Tradition in America* (N.Y., 1955). William E. Leuchtenburg's *Franklin D. Roosevelt: A Profile* (N.Y., 1967) is an excellent collection of essays by leading authorities.

The New Deal Debate

The major references are to: Ernest K. Lindley: *The Roosevelt Revolution, First Phase* (London, 1934); Carl Degler: *Out of Our Past* (rev. ed. N.Y., 1970); E. E. Robinson: *The Roosevelt Leadership 1933-1945* (N.Y., 1955); Barton J. Bernstein ed.: *Towards a New Past: Dissenting Essays in American History* (N.Y., 1968); William A. Williams: *The Contours of American History* (Cleveland, Ohio, 1961); Rexford G. Tugwell: *The Democratic Roosevelt* (N.Y., 1957) and *The Brains Trust* (N.Y., 1968); Herbert Hoover: *The Hoover Memoirs: The Great Depression 1929-1941* (London, 1953) and

Addresses Upon the American Road 1933-1938 (N.Y., 1938); Samuel I. Rosenman: *Working With Roosevelt* (London, 1952); Mario Einaudi: *The Roosevelt Revolution* (N.Y., 1959); Marquis W. Childs: 'They Hate Roosevelt' and Richard L. Neuberger: 'They Love Roosevelt' in Alexander De Conde, Armin Rappaport and William R. Steckel eds: *Patterns in American History* (2 vols Belmont, Calif., 1965); George Wolfskill and J. A. Hudson: *All But the People: Roosevelt and his Critics 1933-1939* (N.Y., 1969).

The Background and Apprenticeship of FDR

For FDR's early life see particularly Freidel, Schlesinger and McGregor Burns *op. cit.;* then: Daniel Fusfeld *The Economic Thought of Franklin D. Roosevelt and the Origins of the New Deal* (N.Y., 1956); Joseph P. Lash: *Eleanor and Franklin* (N.Y., 1971); Eleanor Roosevelt: *This I Remember* (N.Y., 1949); Alfred Rollins Jr: *Roosevelt and Howe* (N.Y., 1962); Samuel Lubell: *The Future of American Politics* (N.Y., 1952); David Burner: *The Politics of Provincialism: The Democratic Party in Transition 1918-1932* (N.Y., 1968); Richard Hofstadter: *The Age of Reform: From Bryan to FDR* (N.Y., 1955).

Governor Roosevelt and New York State, the New Deal in Miniature

The most complete single treatment is Bernard Bellush: *Franklin D. Roosevelt as Governor of New York* (N.Y., 1955). See also John M. Blum: *From the Morgenthau Diaries, 1928-1938* (Boston, 1959), and Eric F. Goldman: *Rendezvous with Destiny: A History of Modern American Reform* (N.Y., 1952). On Hoover see particularly Joan Hoff Wilson: *Herbert Hoover: Forgotten Progressive* (Boston, 1975), J. Joseph Huthmacher and Warren I. Susman: *Herbert Hoover and the Crisis of American Capitalism* (Cambridge, Mass., 1973), Elliott A. Rosen: *Hoover, Roosevelt and the Brains Trust: From Depression to New Deal* (N.Y., 1977), and Albert U. Romasco: *The Poverty of Abundance: Hoover, the Nation and the Depression* (N.Y., 1965). On the Great Depression see Jim Potter: *The American Economy Between the World Wars* (London, 1974); Lester V. Chandler: *America's Greater Depression 1929-1941* (N.Y., 1970) and Studs Terkel: *Hard Times: An Oral History of the Great Depression* (N.Y., 1970). Particularly useful on the election of 1932 are: Roy V. Peel and Thomas Donnelly: *The 1932 Campaign* (N.Y., 1935) and the appropriate sections of Arthur M. Schlesinger Jr, F. L. Israel and W. P. Hansen eds: *A History of American Presidential Elections* (4 vols N.Y., 1971). See also: Harold Gosnell: *Champion Campaigner: Franklin D. Roosevelt* (N.Y., 1952). Interesting political details are to be found in the accounts of FDR's political managers, particularly James A. Farley: *Jim Farley's Story* (N.Y., 1948) and *Behind the Ballots* (N.Y., 1938) and Edward J. Flynn: *You're the Boss* (N.Y., 1947).

A Pragmatic Ideology for the New Deal?

See particularly the relevant volumes of *The Public Papers,* and Thomas H. Greer: *What Roosevelt Thought: The Social and Political Ideas of Franklin D. Roosevelt* (East Lansing, 1958). Also Arthur A. Ekirch Jr: *Ideologies and Utopias: The Impact of the New Deal on American Thought* (Chicago, 1969); Henry Steele Commager: *The American Mind* (New Haven, Conn., 1950);

Walter Lippmann: *The Good Society* (N.Y., 1937); Raymond Moley and E. A. Rosen; *The First New Deal* (N.Y., 1966); Arthur M. Schlesinger, Jr, and Morton White eds.: *Paths of American Thought* (London, 1964); Richard H. Pells: *Radical Visions and American Dreams* (N.Y., 1973); Morton J. Frisch: *Franklin D. Roosevelt: The Contribution of the New Deal to American Political Thought and Practice* (Boston, 1975).

The New Deal in Action

Essential for an understanding of Roosevelt, by an associate who knew him better than most, is Frances Perkins's *The Roosevelt I Knew* (N.Y., 1946). See also Raymond Moley: *After Seven Years* (N.Y., 1939). Most major figures around Roosevelt wrote autobiographical statements and there are a number of excellent biographies, including Searle F. Charles: *Minister of Relief: Harry Hopkins and the Depression* (Syracuse, 1963) and Bernard Sternsher: *Rexford Tugwell and the New Deal* (New Brunswick, 1964). Basil Rauch's *A History of the New Deal 1933-1938* (N.Y., 1944) propounded the theory that there were two New Deals, the first emphasising recovery, the second reform.

On industrial policy see Bernard Bellush: *The Failure of the NRA* (N.Y., 1975); Ellis W. Hawley: *The New Deal and the Problem of Monopoly* (Princeton, 1966). On agriculture there is a voluminous literature including Christiana M. Campbell: *The Farm Bureau and the New Deal* (Urbana, 1962); David E. Conrad: *The Forgotten Farmers: The Story of Sharecroppers and the New Deal* (Urbana, 1965); Sidney Baldwin: *Poverty and Politics: The Rise and Decline of the Farm Security Administration* (Chapel Hill, 1968); Donald H. Grubbs: *Cry From the Cotton: The Southern Tenant Farmers' Union and the New Deal* (Chapel Hill, 1971); Richard S. Kirkendall: *Social Scientists and Farm Politics in the Age of Roosevelt* (Columbia, 1966); John L. Shover: *Cornbelt Rebellion: The Farmer's Holiday Association* (Urbana, 1965); Van L. Perkins: *Crisis in Agriculture: The Agricultural Adjustment Administration and the New Deal, 1933* (Berkeley, 1969). For the Civilian Conservation Corps see the monograph of that title by John A. Salmond (Durham, N.C., 1967). On other New Deal policies see Michael E. Parrish: *Securities Regulation and the New Deal* (New Haven, 1970); Thomas K. McCraw: *TVA and the Power Fight, 1933-1939* (Philadelphia, 1971); Daniel Nelson: *Unemployment Insurance: The American Experience 1915-1935* (Madison, 1968); Paul K. Conkin: *Tomorrow a New World: The New Deal Community Program* (Ithaca, 1959); Arthur J. Altmeyer: *The Formative Years of Social Security* (Madison, 1966); William F. McDonald: *The Federal Relief Administration and the Arts* (Columbus, 1969); Jane De Hart Mathews: *The Federal Theatre 1935-1939* (Princeton, 1967); R. D. McKinzie: *The New Deal for Artists* (Princeton, 1973). New Deal policies towards organised labour deserve special consideration, and a highly selective list must include Milton Derber and Edwin Young eds: *Labour and the New Deal* (Madison, 1957); Walter Galenson: *The CIO Challenge to the AFL* (Cambridge, Mass., 1960); Irving Bernstein: *Turbulent Years: A History of the American Worker, 1933-1941* (Boston, 1969); Jerold S. Auerbach: *Labor and Liberty: The La Follette Committee and the New Deal* (Indianapolis, 1966) and two books by Sidney Fine: *The Automobile Under the Blue Eagle* (Ann Arbor, 1963) and *Sit-Down: The General Motors Strike of 1936-37* (Ann Arbor, 1969); J. Joseph

Huthmacher: *Senator Robert F. Wagner and the Rise of Urban Liberalism* (N.Y., 1968). On the negro during the 1930s the following are indispensable: Raymond Wolters: *The Negroes and the Great Depression* (Westport, 1970); Ralph J. Bunche: *The Political Status of the Negro in the Age of FDR* (Chicago, 1973), and Bernard Sternsher ed.: *The Negro in Depression and War: Prelude to Revolution, 1930-1945* (Chicago, 1969). Some of the opposition to Roosevelt is discussed in George Wolfskill: *The Revolt of the Conservatives: A History of the American Liberty League* (Boston, 1962); David H. Bennett: *Demagogues in the Depression: American Radicals and the Union Party 1932-1936* (New Brunswick. 1969): Donald R. McCoy: *Angry Voices: Left of Center politics in the New Deal Era* (Lawrence, Kansas, 1958); T. Harry Williams: *Huey Long* (New York, 1969); Charles J. Tull: *Father Coughlin and the New Deal* (Syracuse, 1965); James T. Patterson: *Congressional Conservatism and the New Deal* (Lexington, 1967).

Roosevelt the Revolutionary?

The Supreme Court fight is analysed in Robert Jackson: *The Struggle for Judicial Supremacy* (N.Y., 1941) and the Court Packing Plan by William E. Leuchtenburg in *Essays in the New Deal*, ed. by Harold M. Hollingsworth and William F. Holmes (Austin, 1969). Important works on the organisation of government during the New Deal period are A. J. Wann: *The President as Chief Administrator* (Washington, D.C., 1968) and Richard Polenberg: *Reorganizing Roosevelt's Government, 1936-1939* (Cambridge, Mass., 1966). The impact of the complexity of the federal system on the New Deal in operation is brilliantly outlined in James T. Patterson: *The New Deal and the States: Federalism in Transition* (Princeton, 1969).